515
Scrapbooking Ideas

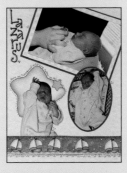

The beginning of the most perfect man began in the most humble of homes.

For Time and all Eternity

How does your Garden grow?

Hi Sunshine!

Inch by inch, row by row, I'm gonna watch my garden grow!

Old Toys

LOOK WHO'S PEEKING UP TO SEE HE'S THREE

IT'S ME !

MOM JUST HAPPENED TO GET ONE PICTURE OF ME, THE REST IS ON VIDEO!

515
Scrapbooking Ideas

Vanessa-Ann

Sterling Publishing Co., Inc., New York
A Sterling/Chapelle Book

Chapelle Ltd.

Owner: Jo Packham

Editor: Gina Swapp

Staff: Marie Barber, Ann Bear, Areta Bingham, Kass Burchett, Rebecca Christensen, Marilyn Goff, Holly Hollingsworth, Susan Jorgensen, Barbara Milburn, Linda Orton, Karmen Quinney, Leslie Ridenour, Cindy Stoeckl

Designers: Becky Hunsaker, Brianna Johnson Shirley Pilkington, Emily Salmond

Library of Congress Cataloging-in-Publication Data

515 scrapbooking ideas / Vanessa Ann.
    p.cm.
  "A Sterling/Chapelle book."
  Includes index
  ISBN 0-8069-4495-1
   1. Photograph albums. 2. Photographs--Conservation and restoration.
3. Scrapbooks. I. Title: Five hundred fifteen scrapbooking ideas. II.
Vanessa-Ann Collection (Firm) III. Title.

TR465.A135 2000
745.593--dc21   99-053583

10 9 8 7 6 5 4 3 2 1

A Sterling/Chapelle Book

Published by Sterling Publishing Company, Inc.
387 Park Avenue South, New York, NY 10016
© 2000 by Chapelle Ltd.
Distributed in Canada by Sterling Publishing
^C/o Canadian Manda Group, One Atlantic Avenue, Suite 105
Toronto, Ontario, Canada M6K 3E7
Distributed in Great Britain and Europe by Cassell PLC
Wellington House, 125 Strand, London WC2R 0BB, England
Distributed in Australia by Capricorn Link (Australia) Pty Ltd.
P.O. Box 6651, Baulkham Hills, Business Centre, NSW 2153, Australia
Printed in China
All Rights Reserved

Sterling ISBN 0-8069-4495-1

If you have any questions or comments, please contact:

Chapelle Ltd., Inc.
P.O. Box 9252
Ogden, UT 84409

Phone: (801) 621-2777
FAX: (801) 621-2788
e-mail: Chapelle@chapelleltd.com

Table of Contents

Introduction

Scrapbooking is a rewarding activity that can be enjoyed by people of any age. It promotes a strong sense of belonging and self-esteem as well as being just plain fun! *515 Scrapbooking Ideas* is designed to stimulate creative ideas for transforming your treasured memories into valuable keepsakes. You will find ideas for pages that are simple and quick as well as those that are elegant and detailed. The techniques showcased here are varied and plentiful, from matting and cropping to stamping and stickers. Enjoy gathering ideas for your own perfect scrapbook pages.

Archival

When you put time and effort into creating scrapbook pages, you want to make certain that your pages will last for many years. The culprit for deteriorating pages is acid. Acid will, over time, eat away at pictures, causing them to become yellow and brittle. All papers used in scrapbooks should be acid-free and lignin-free. On occasion you will want to include items that are not acid-free, such as certificates or awards. These can be displayed in a sheet protector, or sprayed with a buffer spray and mounted onto buffered paper. This will neutralize acid pH levels.

Although a paper may start out acid-free, remember that acid can move into it from other high-acid objects in contact with it, from environmental pollutants or even from contact with oil in human hands.

Pens and adhesives, stickers and any other embellishments also need to be acid-free. *Be a label reader to make certain your pages will stand the test of time.*

Supplies

These basic supplies will help you create a perfect memory.

ACID-FREE PAPERS - will add color and dimension to your pages. Card stock is the most widely used paper and comes in different weights and sizes. Analyze what will go

on your page to determine whether to use lightweight, medium-weight, or heavy-weight card stock. It also comes in hundreds of colors and textures. Use card stock for background sheets, mats, die-cuts, or with craft punches.

Give variety to your pages by using patterned, bordered, or textured papers. Decorative or novelty papers and stationery are often used for backgrounds. They also can be cut out to enhance photos, make borders and mats, or create patterns.

ADHESIVES - can include acid-free double-sided tape, glue sticks, neutral pH adhesive, double-sided adhesive foam dots and tabs. Spray adhesive that has been specially designed for adhering photos onto scrapbook pages is quite popular as well.

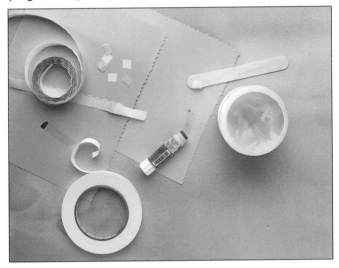

CUTTING TOOLS - are essential to enable you to always have clean crisp lines. A large pair of craft scissors works well for general cutting, while a small pair makes small detailed cutting much easier.

A craft knife with a replaceable blade can be very useful in cutting straight edges and tight corners cleanly. A paper trimmer or a rotary cutter are also helpful in making straight, clean lines.

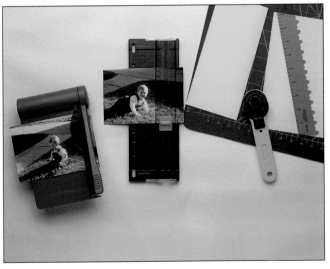

Decorative-edged scissors are a fun way to cut backgrounds, mats, or make creative accents for your pages. They come in a large variety of edges. As you begin, you may want to try those of a fellow scrapbooker. Then you can purchase the designs that you like best.

PENS AND MARKERS - should be archival quality for labeling, highlighting, decorating, and journaling. A fine-tip permanent pen works best for journaling, fine lines, and tiny accents. Broader tipped markers and calligraphy pens work well for titles or enhancing around photos. Use a variety of colors to give interest to your pages.

A pen is available that can take "red eye" out of photos and help to make photos more

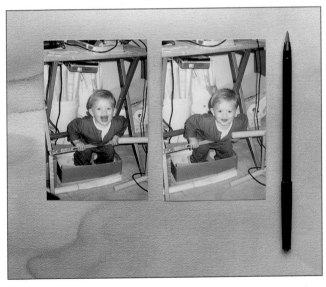

attractive. Colored pencils may also be used to add variety to pages and enhance photos. Be certain they are water-resistant.

A white opaque pen works great on dark papers and can give a whole new look to a page. Metallic pens of gold or silver can easily add a little sparkle or a finishing touch, while a photo-safe pencil is designed specifically for labeling your photos. It can also be used to trace a template onto the photo without damaging it.

could be used for a family album and perhaps a different size for individuals. You can purchase one, make one, or just add to one that is not quite all you want. Think about whether you want all of them to match or if you prefer them all to be different. A series of look-alike books can tell a continuing story or share a special event.

SHEET PROTECTORS - will protect scrapbook pages and keep photos on facing pages from rubbing together. Sheet protectors come in different weights and finishes, from non-glare to high gloss. The choice is a personal preference but should stay consistent within your scrapbook. Make certain to purchase archival quality.

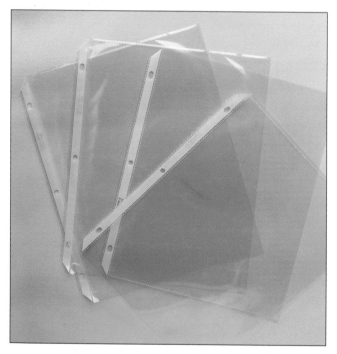

Miscellaneous

PHOTO ALBUMS - come in a variety of styles and sizes, so your imagination can take over when you select yours. Find a book that suits your personality and style.

The main differences between albums are the binding and the size. Most scrapbookers use a simple 3-ring binding, an expandable binding, or a bound album. Album bindings should allow scrapbook pages to lay flat.

Album pages come in a variety of sizes from very small to quite large, the most common being 8 1/2" X 11" and 12" X 12". You may decide to use several sizes. One size

Other available supplies include: stamps, punches, die-cuts, templates, clip art, photo corners, rulers, and stickers. These are available at local craft stores. Be certain to check labels to ensure that everything is acid-free, then let your imagination go wild!

Photographs

Great scrapbooks start with great photos. Although professional photographs are a wonderful addition to a scrapbook, spontaneous personal snapshots capture unforgettable moments forever. The more scrapbooking you do, the better your photography will become. Pay close attention to the viewfinder on your camera, and crop out unnecessary background. For variety, use a different angle on a shot. Photos of children are often better if taken on the child's level. Do not be afraid to try new angles, and take more than one shot of your subject. Getting double prints of your photos is always a good idea. Remember, practice makes perfect!

CROPPING PHOTOS - will enhance a photograph and can make the subjects appear closer. Many times a photo has too much background or foreground. When cropping photos, use a paper trimmer or rotary cutter to take out unwanted sections of your photos, or use fun shapes that will complement your page. Use a template and a photo-safe pencil to trace the template onto your photo. Cookie cutters make great templates.

Cropping is a completely safe technique for your photos, but remember that it is irreversible. If you need to crop an irreplaceable one-of-a-kind photograph, consider making and cropping a color copy. It is recommended

that you do not crop an instant photo. Make color copies of instant photos, then crop as desired.

You may also consider silhouetting a photo—trimming around the subjects, following their contours. This is not for every page or photo, but sometimes silhouetting enhances the page and the photo, and enables you to place more photos on a page. Take your time and use a small pair of scissors with a slender blade so that you can cut around corners and delicate areas. Be particularly careful when you cut around hair to ensure that heads are not misshapen.

MATTING PHOTOS - is a simple thing to do. Most photos look better when they are surrounded with a little bit of color or decoration. Matting will accent your photo and enhance your entire page. Select an archival paper or card stock that is complementary to your photo and page background. Cut the paper to be used for matting larger than your photo and adhere the photo onto the paper. Patterned papers make attractive mats as well as solid papers. Try matting a round-cropped photo onto a square mat. Precut mats are available at craft stores and make an attractive accent to a photo. Cutting mats with decorative-edged scissors or using double or triple mats will add variety to your photos and pages.

Journaling

Journaling is documenting photos by either handwriting or lettering names, dates, and events (the who, what, where, when, and why) on the background paper. The writing on a page will help explain the subject or event more clearly. Writing personal feelings and captions about the subject gives pages added value and interest. Include family stories, poems, and songs that correspond with the photos. A child's first words or favorite phrase enhances priceless photos.

Lettering is a creative way of decorating and accenting pages. The text becomes an element of the page design, drawing attention to the words as well as the photos. There are unlimited styles to choose from and craft stores have books available to give you ideas. Experiment on scratch paper and come up with your own unique style. Write your title or lettering in the desired style on the page first in pencil, then go over the pencil with a pen or marker.

Adhesive lettering is another way to create a unique message for your pages. Different styles can be mixed and matched to produce a truly personalized message or title.

Ideas from Brianna

Brianna Johnson started scrapbooking four years ago when her first child was born. It was such a joy for her to capture moments of life that she never wanted to forget. Instead of keeping a journal, she makes scrapbooks. She has one book for each year of each of her children's lives.

Recently, Brianna started her own professional photography business, which she finds both challenging and rewarding. She is very active and one of her favorite sports is rock climbing.

Brianna, her husband Ryan, and their children Cloe (4), and Gavin (1) all enjoy looking back at their memories again and again because they are recorded in scrapbooks.

• It is important to include some of your own handwritten script in your scrapbooks because it personalizes the memories and your personality shows through.

• Try to write a letter to each of your children each year and put it in the front of their scrapbooks. Write about all that has happened during the past year and what you hope for the next year. It is important to express your feelings about each child. These will be treasured for many years.

• If you have a lot of memorabilia that is hard to put in your scrapbook, but you want it in your book, take a picture of it and make pages from the photographs. Then you can store your memorabilia or throw it away.

• Use extra pictures by cutting out around faces and making a collage page.

• When someone says something humorous, write it down and transfer it onto your pages. It is fun to go back and remember events or situations.

• Create your own backgrounds with scraps of patterned or colored paper.

• It is fun to have young children make a scrapbook page of their own. Give them some extra pictures and supplies and let them be creative. You can put their pages in a book of their "very first scrapbook pages".

• Ribbons are a fun addition to any scrapbook page. Remember that everything in your book does not have to be paper.

...1ST BATH IN YOUR LITTLE YELLOW "TUBBY"...

...TESS KHEIL GAVE IT TO YOU!

...YOU DON'T LIKE BATHS AT ALL...

...YOU SCREAM THE ENTIRE TIME...

...YOU LOVE HAVING YOUR HAIR WASHED!

...2 DAYS OLD...

JANUARY 21st 1995

5¢

you've got the cutest little baby face!

How does your Garden grow?

Hi Sunshine!

Inch by inch, row by row, I'm gonna watch my garden grow!

12

*you lift your head
while laying
on your stomach*

two months

*you laugh
and coo,
especially
at gravity*

*you smile
when spoken
to*

DR. FRANK BROWN

2 MONTH CHECK-UP!!!

YOUR VERY FIRST DOCTOR! HE IS
SUCH A GOOD, GENUINE PERSON.
EACH TIME WE WOULD GO IN FOR
A CHECK UP, HE WOULD SPEND
AT LEAST 15 MINUTES WITH US,
ASKING ME HOW OUR LIVES WERE.
HE ALWAYS HAD GREAT ADVICE
FOR US TOO! WE ARE BLESSED
TO HAVE HIM FOR OUR DOCTOR.

When laying out scrapbook pages, make certain to leave room for journaling. You may think that journaling isn't necessary because you would never forget the event, but remember, your scrapbooks will be passed from generation to generation. The information you supply will be very important to others viewing the pages and is a necessary part of any scrapbook page. Journaling "tells the story". Even a few years can make a difference in what you will remember.

The doctor visits documented here are things a child would never know about if the visits were not recorded. Journaling can be short and simple like the example above left, or a little more detailed as in the examples to the right. Sometimes simple words used to title pages will tell about the subject, as in the above right example of Dr. Frank Brown.

Cloé

8 months old

*You are beginning to
become very active, you
are reacting to people,
crawling everywhere,
and trying to walk.
It is very fun to take
pictures of you because
you love the camera so
much. You are such a
beautiful baby. People
comment about you
wherever we go. You
can walk holding on
to furniture. You love
to play pat-a-cake
and make noise by
banging two objects
together. You also can
understand small words
like no and bye-bye.*

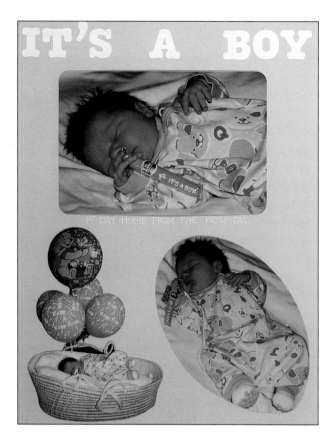

Mix different techniques on a page. Silhouetting and matting are the perfect compliment to each other (above & below).

The jagged edge of the decorative-edged scissors (above) complements the messy hairdo.

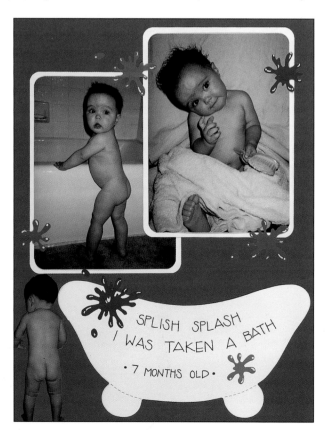

Laying out double-page spreads allows you more room to work with a theme. It can also give variety to your album and makes it pleasing to the eye as you flip through.

Double-page spreads can be a continuation as shown above or just two pages with a similar theme as shown on page 15.

MANY TIMES A DANDELION IS A WEED IN THE GREEN, GRASSY SOD. BUT A DANDELION IS A FLOWER DIVINE IN THE HANDS OF A CHILD OF GOD.

24 KARAT CLOÉ

CLOÉ & UNCLE JOSH

·PLAYING IN THE
WATER ON A HOT SUMMERS DAY·

To accommodate more than one large photo on a page, consider overlapping or mounting them at angles. Bleeding photos off the page is another idea.

18

Stationery can be cut apart and used as a frame or as stickers (above).

Crop photos and use them to create fun shapes (below).

Crop photos to match page. The photo (above) is cut straight and complements the pine trees' straight lines.

Rounded corners on the photo (above) add to the soft, curved lines of the cut-out tulips.

Try journaling around cut-out shapes or stickers (above and below).

Just a few well-placed stickers give a little pizzazz to a page (above).

Random stickers are a fun way to accent a theme page (above).

Mats are a great way to tie several pages together (above and below).

WHAT A SPECIAL YEAR WE HAVE HAD! CLOÉ YOU ARE SUCH AN ANGEL IN MY LIFE. BEING YOUR MOTHER HAS BROUGHT ME SUCH HAPPINESS & GREAT JOY! I LOVE THIS TIME OF YEAR TO REFLECT BACK ON THOSE YEARS THAT HAVE PAST, ESPECIALLY THIS LAST YEAR & ALSO THE YEAR CHRIST WAS BORN. I LOVE THE SAVIOR CLOÉ & I KNOW THAT HE LOVES YOU. ALWAYS KEEP HIM IN YOUR HEART!

Stickers can be used in many ways to add variety or a special effect to a page. In the example below stickers are used to accent a photo. The page to the left uses stickers to decorate and draw your eye smoothly from one photograph to the next. The page on the lower left uses a single sticker in conjunction with other cutouts.

On page 24 (upper left) the stickers make a train track border as well as the train and the smoke. This works great with the photos from the park train ride. The page on the upper right uses stickers to help form a border. The double-page spread (below) uses stickers to form the words "Happy Birthday". Stickers can be used to form any word or name for any page. Mix different letter styles in words for a different look. Be creative with stickers, mix-and-match them with punches, mats, stationery, or cutouts.

CLOE AND HER CHRISTMAS CHOO CHOO

Austin
Chase
Mitch
Heather
Aubrey
Kaden
Hanna
Cloe

HAPPY BIRTHDAY

HAPPY BIRTHDAY

ONE

YEAR

OLD

WHAT A FUN PARTY WE HAD! ALL OF OUR FRIENDS CAME AND WE ATE HOAGIE SANDWICH'S, CHIPS, SALADS AND OF COURSE YOUR BEAR BIRTHDAY CAKE. THERE WAS LOTS OF KIDS SO YOU ALL JUST PLAYED WITH YOUR NEW TOYS & THE BIRTHDAY BALOONS. THE ADULTS JUST ATE AND TALKED FOR HOURS! IT WAS A VERY SPECIAL NIGHT! I THINK WE ALL HAD A GREAT TIME!

I'M ONE

BIRTHDAY PARTY WITH FRIENDS JAN. 21st 1995

CLOE
ONE YEAR OLD

Cropping and silhouetting are fun techniques to mix. When cropping, be certain to include things that help tell the story, such as the flags and balloons on these pages.

Remember to use everyday events in your books as well as special events. "Wash day" (above) is a priceless memory.

Be certain to include special pets in your memories. Take pictures of your children with their favorite furry friend (above).

coloring eggs

easter 1999

Happy
Valentine's
Day

FROM
ME

I love you

FOR VALENTINES DAY
THIS YEAR YOU GAVE
OUT SUZY ZOO CARDS
WITH SWEETHEARTS &
CHOCOLATE LIPS!!!
LOVE

BEAR LAKE '96

HAPPY EASTER

HIPPITY HOP   HIPPITY HOP

PUT ON YOUR DANCIN' SHOES

SPRING DANCE RECITAL '97

° CLOÉ AND CHELSEA °

° CHEEK TO CHEEK °

° A KISS FOR GOOD LUCK °

TAKE A BOW!

Several snapshots of the same occasion can create a sequential picture (below).

Backgrounds cropped from photos can be cut into other shapes or letters (below).

28

A child's handprint adds a lovely touch to your page. Paint the hand with acrylic paint, and press it on your page (above).

You can draw attention to a favorite photo by keeping it larger and placing it on a page all its own (above).

MOMMY, DADDY, & CLOÉ
⭐ JULY 24ᵀᴴ ⭐
WEBER STATE
FIREWORKS!

HELP PREVENT
FOREST FIRES, NEVER
PLAY WITH MATCHES

SMOKEY

KNOTTSBERRY FARM

SMOKEY & ME

AMIGO AUSTIN

AMIGO HUNTER

AMIGO KADEN

CLOÉ

MY THREE AMIGOS

Keep the focus on your photos with simple backgrounds (below).

Close-up snapshots will help preserve memories of special people (below).

31

Celebrate special holidays and occasions by remembering to include special friends and extended family members in your photographs and scrapbook pages (above and below).

You loved to go and visit Santa at the mall and tell him all of your wishes that you have for christmas. This year the thing you wanted most of all is was a red jeep and a kitty. Santa asked you if you had been good throughout the year and you said yes, I am always good!

HOLLYDAYS

CHRISTMAS '96
HAPPY HOLIDAYS
GOING TO SEE
THE LIGHTS

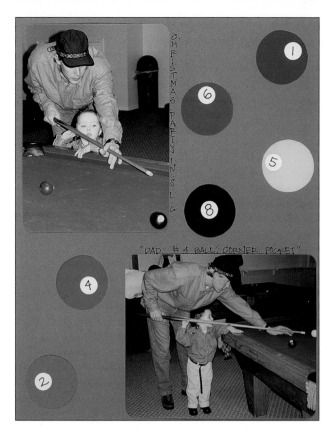

Words as well as photographs can make a unique page. Words can carry special memories about family events (below).

When taking photographs, get close to your subject. Fill the frame so less cropping is necessary (below).

34

Black and white photographs add variety and interest (above).

Cropping several poses into shapes creates a unique page (below).

35

i'm a little doll

Take photos from a variety of angles. The view from baby's feet is a fresh, unique angle (above).

Matting cropped photographs adds a finishing touch (below). Use paper that complements the photos and background.

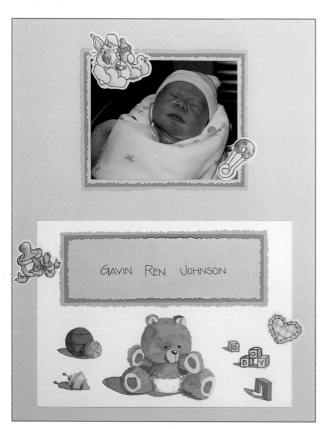

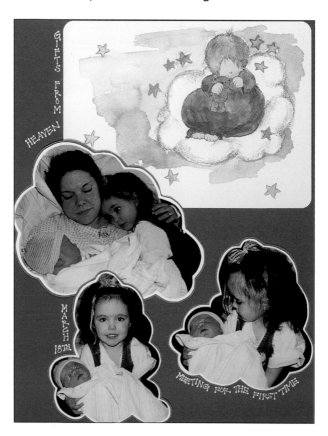

37

Decorative-edged scissors can add a little spice to a scrapbook page. They can be used to cut mats as well as to crop photos.

For a charming, different effect, try mixing a silhouetted photo with cutouts or stickers (below).

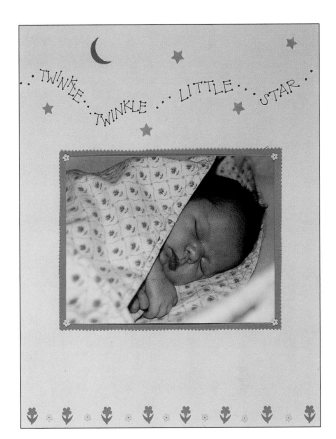

Simple ovals and circles are useful in making faces the focus of attention. Experiment with different sizes (above and below).

Explore the possibilities of a page where data can be added (below) and you can "track" a child's progress or change.

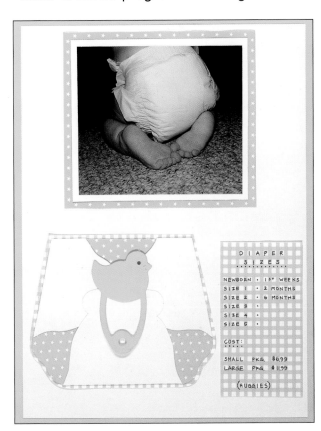

GAVIN · MANDEE · CLOÉ

JUMPIN PALS

Hoppy Easter

SOMEBUNNY SPECIAL

EASTER 1999

JOHNSONS

plant smiles
grow giggles
harvest love

before

gavin march '99

jumping
on the
trampoline

after

Pages don't need to have dozens of photographs to capture a priceless moment.

Double or triple mats are an easy way to highlight a single photograph (below).

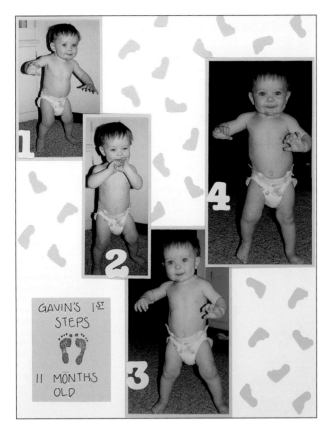

Be certain to have your camera readily available for those once in a lifetime shots (above).

Don't forget to include pages that will bring back fun memories without the use of a photograph (above).

Remember that color is a terrific way to accent your memories. Use black to emphasize the subject (above right), or orange (below) to accent a double-page spread.

Ideas from Emily

A stay-at-home Mom, Emily lives in Ogden, Utah, with her husband and baby boy, Lazarus. She has always enjoyed activities that challenged her creativity, including writing. Growing up in a family of seamstresses, artists, and multitalented people, her life was centered around art.

When Emily was introduced to scrapbooking, it did not take long for her to fall headfirst into a lifelong hobby. She has found a way to express herself and share her memories with family members and friends in the form of photographs and scrapbooks.

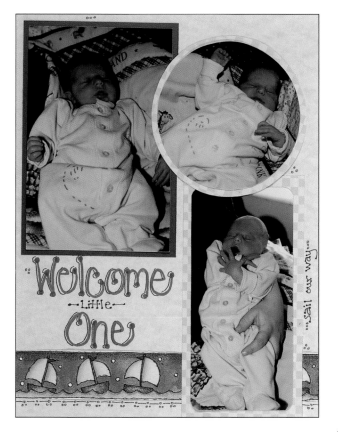

• Patterned papers are quite versatile. They can be used for background papers, making borders, mats for photos or pages, or making cut-out shapes for accents or decorations.

• Cutting out pictures from stationery or patterned papers allows you to make your own stickers.

• Silhouetting a photograph and then using custom-cut objects to go with it or around it will make a unique page.

• Choose mats for photographs that will complement the subject. You may need to try several colors to find just the right one. Double or triple mats will make a photograph really stand out.

45

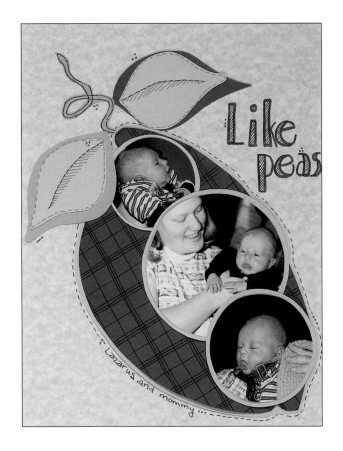

Nature provides an endless number of possibilities for fun scrapbook pages. The pea pods (above) could be any vegetable and the stars (below) provide a fun page theme.

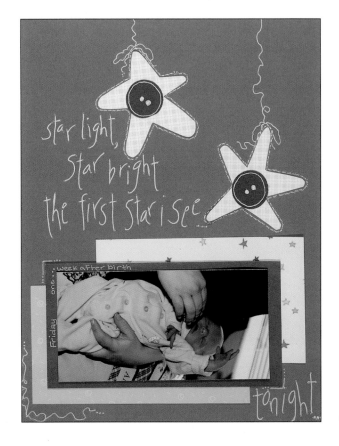

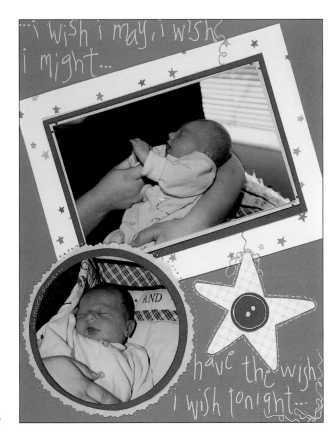

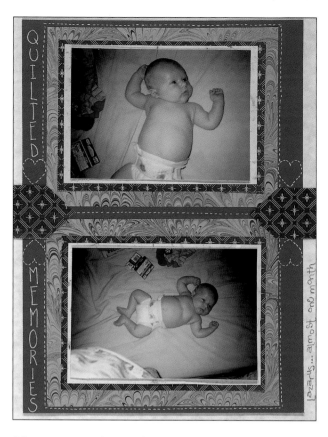

Mats are an inventive way to make a page look quilted (above).

Mats do not have to be cut square. Use other shapes (below) for a unique, look.

We can give our children

one is roots...

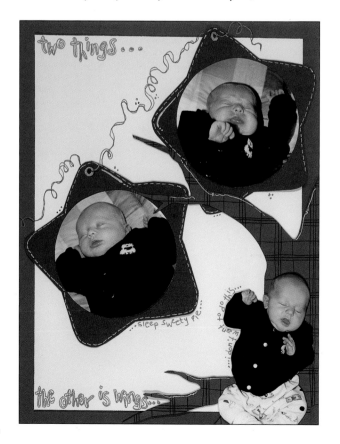

two things...

...sleep sweety pie...

the other is wings...

Scissors and patterned paper provide all the decoration for these pages.

Mix and match template shapes when cropping photos (below).

Using colorful patterned paper will add spice and give variety to your pages. The patterned paper on these pages was not only used to mat the photographs, but was also cut into fun shapes to accent and decorate.

Silhouetting a photograph, then adding custom cutouts creates a special effect.

Fine-tipped pens are great tools to add accents, fine lines, and journaling.

Double-page spreads are a fun way to use several photographs of the same occasion or that have a similar theme.

Patterned paper has an unlimited number of possibilities for creating a scrapbook page. Be certain you have a pair of small craft scissors so you can cut details and very small shapes. In the upper-left page, the paper was cut into a pumpkin shape. The photographs were then cropped into the same shape. The same patterned paper worked well for leaves in the adjoining page.

Often, a fun custom shape can be cut from scraps that you already have and eliminates the need to purchase stickers. The horse on the page to the right was cut from scraps of background paper. The mane and saddle were also cut from colored scrap paper. The mat was cut with decorative-edged scissors, which adds a little extra emphasis to the photograph. Save scraps and organize them in colors or patterns for easy reference.

Cutting the mat and cropping the photograph in the same shape as the subject of the photograph makes these pages eye catching and pleasing to look at.

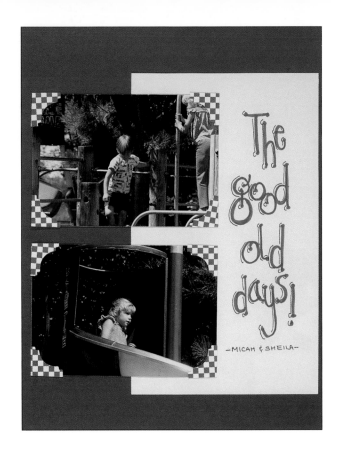

Putting a title on a page (above) will help to bring back memories.

Pens can be used to embellish an entire page (above).

54

Abstract or geometric shapes are a fun way to add accents to your page (above).

Ants (below) are only one insect that can help embellish the memories of a vacation.

You can use color to emphasize a photograph. Color can also be used to complement the subject of photographs, re-create a season, or convey a feeling or mood.

Bleed a graphic onto two pages (above) for an effective way to tie two pages together.

Use acid-free markers to embellish pages with your personal handwriting (above).

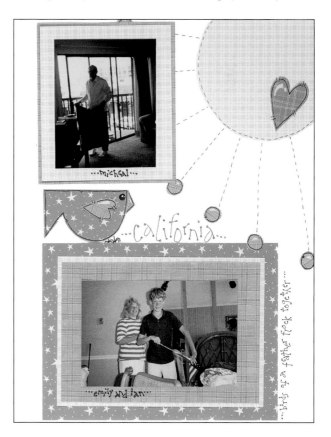

Animals are a favorite to use in decorating scrapbook pages (above). They can be used as an embellishment or as a subject.

Adding a mat or a border is a simple way to finish a page or tie it to another one (below).

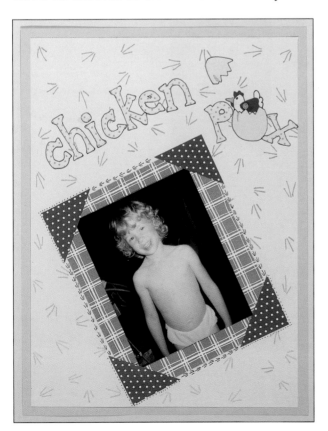

as old as the trees

micah's in white shirt

as old as the hills

Sisters are Forever

california 1992

...california with just the girls

mary   sheila   sharon   emily

Pastel patterns are mixed and matched in these pages to give them a soft fresh look.

Accent cutouts or create cheerful titles with markers or pens.

A single strip of patterned paper ties the pages together (above).

Hand-cut corners are a unique way to finish off a page (below).

Family events, whether large or small, create memories that should be recorded.

For extra emphasis, try double- or triple-matting photographs with patterned paper.

Including snapshots of your home is a good way to recall memories (above).

Bleeding an element across a background ties a double-page spread together (below).

Decorative-edged scissors were used to cut the foil paper mat (below).

Using a metallic pen for journaling or embellishing adds a little extra flair.

Try different lettering styles to write titles and names (above and below).

The snowflakes (above) have been matted to achieve a fun 3D effect.

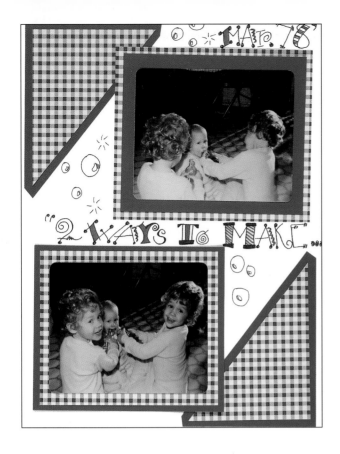

To add a little variety, try mounting pictures horizontally on the page (below).

Be creative with lettering. Try a sentence that spans a double-page spread (above).

Holidays provide a great opportunity to be creative. Double-page spreads give you plenty of room to develop the theme and still highlight those special photographs.

Ideas from Becky

Becky Hunsaker started scrapbooking in 1995 after the loss of an infant son. She wanted to do a special book in his memory and also continue the memories with her two other sons. She was instantly hooked and since that times has completed many books, including a 50th anniversary book for her parents, a book for her husband, a grandpa book, a family photo book, and of course, she continues to work on her children's books. She hopes one day to do her own!

Becky works at Memories by Design, where she teaches a Scrapbook Basics class. She likes to create fun, simple pages that do not detract from the photos. She also loves to add simple verses or journal entries to her pages.

Her other hobbies include sewing, reading, bowling, and spending time with her family. She has experienced many emotions through scrapbooking —from the healing of a broken heart to the excitement of learning more about her heritage, to the thrill of hearing the giggles of her boys as they look at their books.

• Find cute graphics from computer clip art programs and print them on different colors of paper. Cut them apart, then stack them together for a layered effect.

• When I back my pictures or use stencil letters, I use the same pattern paper but in different colors.

• Interview your children or a family member and do a page on their answers. For example a "Favorites at Five" page would feature their favorite color, food, friend, toy, etc. This would also work great for a grandparent.

• Make page pockets to store special notes or pictures in. Use a full piece of card stock for the backing. Then cut stationery or another piece of card stock in half and glue it on three sides to the back piece. This creates a pocket to store special things in. I like to do this for school memorabilia, such as notes from teachers, report cards, or hand-drawn pictures.

• It is interesting to find different ways to use punches. Make a face with the circle punch and use a leaf or scallop punch for the hair. Cut the heart punch in half to make leaves for a flower.

• Stickers can be used to make borders. Place stickers across or down to make an edge to a page.

• Make color copies of blankets, scout badges, kids' pictures, etc., to add to pages. These can be used as backgrounds or just cut out to add accents.

68

Colored paper scraps created the background (above) to match the photograph.

This black-and-white photo is complement-
ed by a handmade paper mat (above).

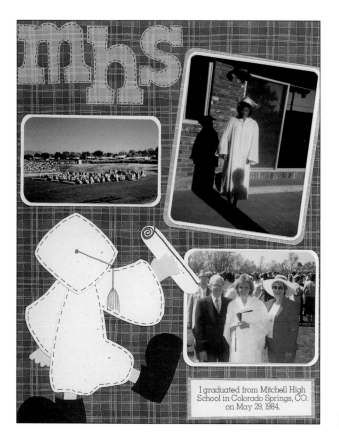

69

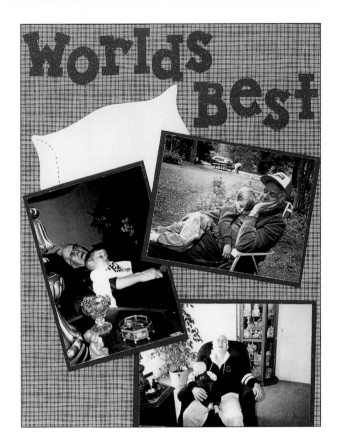

Each of the these photographs were taken at different times, but they complement each other wonderfully in this delightful double-page spread (above).

Stationery can be cut out and used as a border (above), or cut out and used as a picture frame (below).

Die-cuts are a playful way to decorate and come in a variety of shapes to coordinate with any page.

Cropping photos in circles works great with a button theme (above).

Journaling can be done with sticker letters (above) or by hand (below).

In these four examples, background papers were used and journaling was added by hand or printed on a computer.

Some photos won't need a mat (lower left) while others look great with a single (lower right) or double mat (above pages).

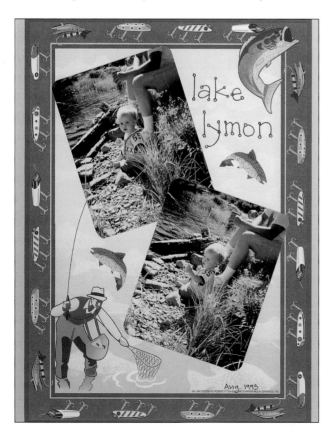

73

Punches and die-cuts are very versatile. In the page below, balloon die-cuts were used as an accent and the cupcake for journaling. In the lower-right page a leaf punch was used to punch out leaves from the background paper. Small squares of complementary colors were then glued to the background paper to fill in the "holes" with color. Other leaves were punched to embellish the photographs and the rest of the page. The letters were also cut from colored paper and added for the title. To finish off the page, decorative-edged scissors made a perfect edge for the photograph mats.

On the opposite page (upper right), the snowflake punches are placed over and under the photographs. This serves as a snowy mat for the photographs and gives the illusion of snow falling. Think of other creative ways to use punches.

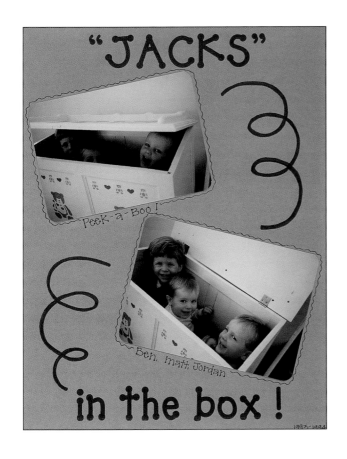

"JACKS"

Peek-a-Boo!

Ben, Matt, Jordan

in the box !

1993-1994

SNOW

march 9

HAPPY EASTER

Annual Neighborhood Easter Egg Hunt

April 1994

PJ's

Print-out titles or graphics on a comptuer before adding photographs (above and below).

Try matting titles or letters on your pages. The letters (above) were hand-cut. The caption (below)was printed on the computer.

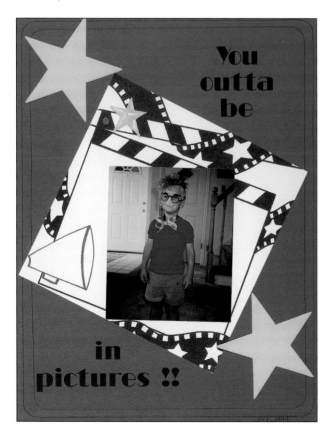

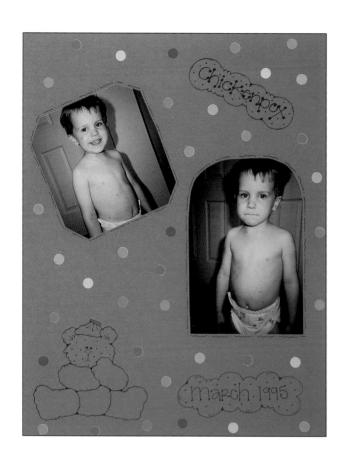

Chickenpox

March 1995

Gone Fishin'

The Fish Farm

Jordan's first preschool field trip was to the fish farm. All the kids caught a fish to bring home but the best memory was teacher Michelle falling in the lake to catch one of the fish that almost got away!!

· Jordan· Ben· Ashley· Adam· Andrew· Dane·

Jordan's Big Catch of the Day!!

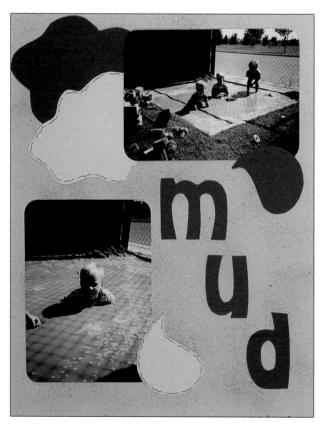

mud

It's a Hoe Down

Party

With the Hunsakers--1995

Where is Tom Sawyer when you need him?

Painting the shed!

West Yellowstone Grizzly Discovery Center. Aug. 1995

Golf... Golf...

"Nice chip shot ▷"

"FORE!"

3

PGA here I come ▷

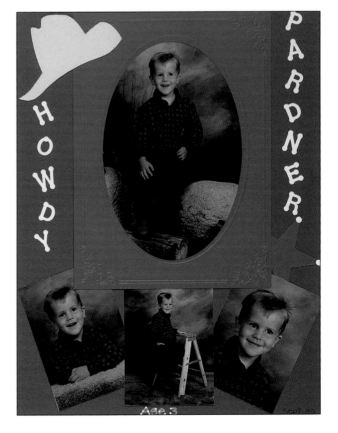

HOWDY

PARDNER.

Age 3

Photographs can be adhered to your pages in a number of ways. The method you choose depends on the photograph and the subject.

On the opposite page, the upper-right page was put together with a prepackaged kit. The lower-right page used professional portraits and a precut mat. This page was enhanced by using several poses from the portraits taken, die-cuts, and sticker letters. The upper- and lower-left pages were mounted without mats and the corners were rounded.

The page to the left uses silhouetting to make the subject the focus of the page. This is a terrific technique that requires a small pair of craft scissors or craft knife to make detailed intricate cuts. Below, the photographs have been single-matted. Experiment with different ways to mount your photographs.

When you have several snapshots of a memorable event, make a collage (above).

Items other than photographs give a page sentimental value (below).

Some photographs include scenery that is important to the event (above), and don't require cropping.

Remember that colors can be used to accentuate a photograph or to complement an entire page.

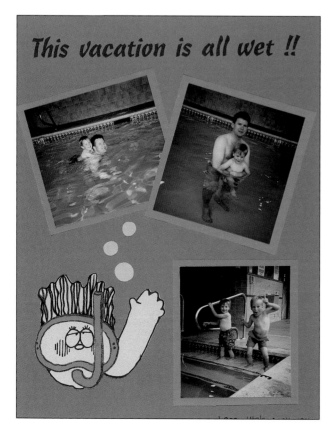

Countless background papers are available that make putting a page together as easy as adding a title and photographs. They work well for single or double pages.

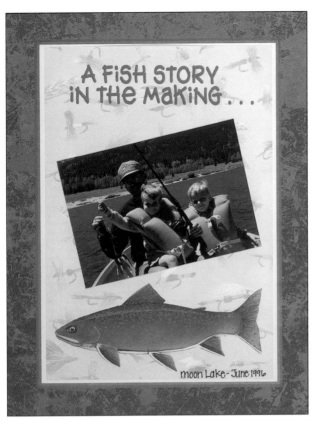

Enhance school pictures with computer printouts and stickers.

Not so great photographs can be an excellent way to preserve family memories.

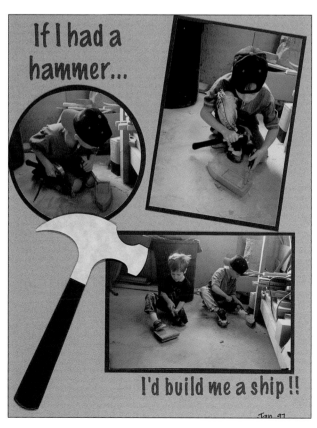

83

Children are
God's way of
telling us
that
tomorrow
will be
beautiful.

Journaling does not have to be facts or titles. A poem or quote can add sentimental value (above).

Jordans first year of T-Ball 1997

HOMERUN

Jordan Hunsaker '97
Pitcher

Background paper can be used as it comes packaged (above), or cut out and used to decorate a page (below).

It's a sleepover party !!

The gang all got together for a sleepover at the Halversons. We really didn't get much sleep but we sure did have a fun time !!

The Green Dragons

Region 239 AYSO 1997

Coaches: Larry Hunsaker, Darren Smith
Clayton Mabrey, Daniel Moyes, Jordan Hunsaker, Taylor Smith
Trevor Knowlton, Nick Romney, Anthony Bassett, Kyle Harvey
Missing: Kyle Ortega, JayDee Germer, Michael Collins

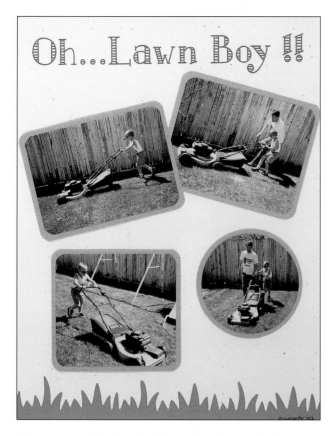

You can add simple lines to die-cuts to strengthen their look (below).

Coloring black-and-white clip art (above) enhances the look of the page.

Notice the variety of ways to create a page about water and swimming.

Print a graphic on several colors, cut them apart, then adhere in layers (below).

Double-page spreads don't have to end with double pages. They can extend onto other pages to include an entire vacation or family event. Use lettering and color to tie them all together.

Don't be afraid to overlap graphics with your photographs, it will add interest to your page (above and below).

Computers offer not only access to graphics and artwork but also offer a wide variety of fonts (above and below).

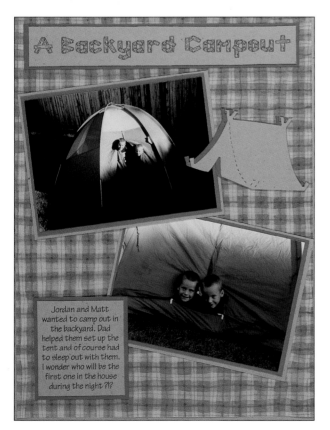

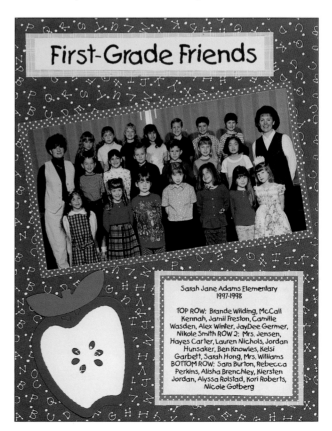

These pages use double and triple mats, punches, stickers, coordinating colors, computer-generated and handwritten lettering. Don't be afraid to mix techniques.

FALL

We took our annual fall drive with Havilands, Halleys and Knowles to find and look at the beautiful fall leaves.

"FALLING" INTO FUN !!

NINJA BOYS

Happy Halloween... Oct. 1997

First Grade Halloween Parade and Party

Clowning around with Mrs. Jensen

Jordan, Alex, Ben & Becky

Try tilting or overlapping photographs. This will add interest and variety to your pages. Accents and borders can also overlap as shown in this double-page spread (above).

A smile
from a
child is
packaged
sunshine &
rainbows !!

Matt's last day of Preschool
May 29, 1998

Torn white paper and a stationery cutout help this page look like the perfect tubing hill (above).

Remember that you can include items in your scrapbook that help others visualize the story (below).

TUCKETT'S FARM
Preschool Fieldtrip
May 1998

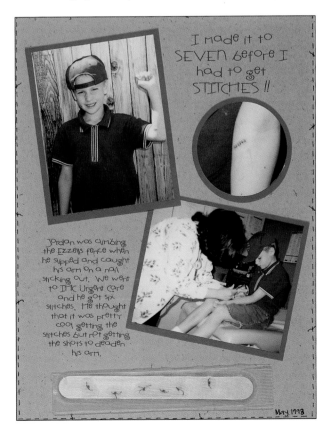

I made it to
SEVEN before I
had to get
STITCHES !!

Jordan was climbing
the Ezzells fence when
he slipped and caught
his arm on a nail
sticking out. We went
to IHC Urgent Care
and he got six
stitches. He thought
that it was pretty
cool getting the
stitches but not getting
the shots to deaden
his arm.

May 1998

Use patterned papers to give added interest to double or triple mats on a photograph or a double-matted page (below).

Photographs of favorite hobbies as well as special events help to preserve a variety of special memories (above and below).

Storyteller for a Day

In first grade Jordan was given the assignment to be a storyteller for the day. He got to sit in the 'story' rocker and read a book to his class. He picked one on baseball, so of course he had to wear his T-ball uniform while he read it.

June 24, 1998

It's-a-pizza party !!

Jordans first grade class had an end of the year pizza party. They had fun making their own pizza and even ended up with flour on their noses.

Patting out the dough... well trying anyways !!

Putting on as many toppings that will fit and then some...

The finished masterpiece !!

June 30, 1998

Add your own personal feelings about the subjects on your page. It will mean a lot to those who see your pages in the future.

Beary Best Friends
Jordan and Hunter

Spontaneous shots of siblings become precious keepsakes (above), but don't forget the posed group shots (below).

Great joy comes in seeing our family enter another generation.

Family Reunion

93

One of life's little pleasures...

...walking in my Grandpa's footsteps.

June 1996

I love you THIS much !!

Matt, Bobbi, Jordan

Aug '98

Using a complementary background with journaling creates a mood (above).

Whenever possible try to leave a date on your page for future reference (below).

rocks for sale 25.¢

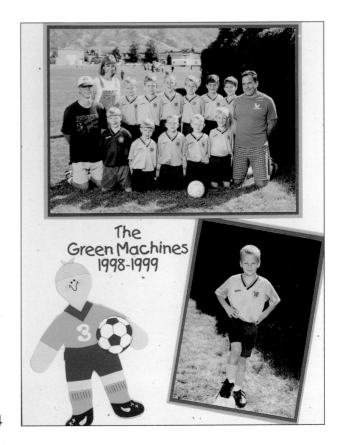

The Green Machines 1998-1999

Stickers are available in any shape or form you can think of. Use them to accent or to create an entire page (below).

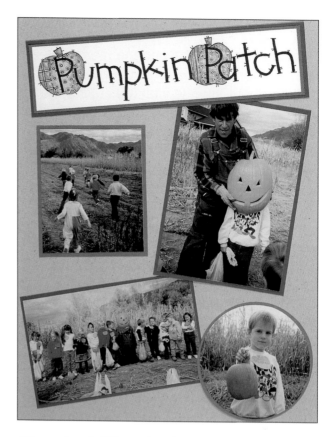

Die-cuts of different colors, cut apart, then pieced together make a bright multicolored graphic (below).

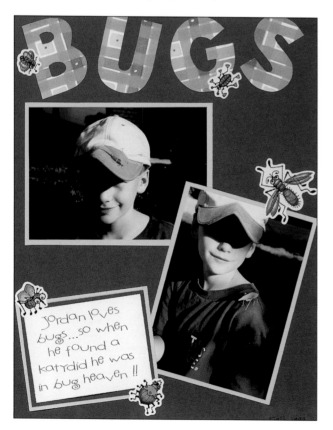

Your photographs and the memories behind them are precious. Journaling, or writing about them is vital to keeping the memories alive. Although the details and dates may seem very clear at the present time, they won't be in a few years. Be certain to include names, dates, and places wherever appropriate. These statistics are the easiest to forget. Try to recall feelings as well as facts so that others who see your pages in the future will have a better understanding of the events shared on your pages.

The page to the right needs only a brief explanation to summarize the hunting trip. On the opposite page (upper left) a slightly longer paragraph gives the details of the forgotten lunch box. The brief journaling on the upper-right and lower-left pages utilize fun fonts from a computer. The pages below use only a playful title.

A Hunting We Will Go...

Larry took Jordan on his first hunting trip October 1998. They came home empty handed because Jordan got tooo tired half way up the mountain. They still made fun memories together though.

Girls Just

TRICK OR TREAT!

Halloween '98

Wanna Have Fun!

The Forgotten Lunch Box...

Jordan was always forgetting one of his two lunch boxes at school. After forgetting both lunch boxes, mom was teasing him about it and he said, "I'm just a little boy with a little brain!! I have to remember to get up in the morning and get dressed, I have to go to school and remember everything to do there, I have to remember to come home and play and do all those other things and you want me to remember my lunchbox!!"
March 1999
Age 8

The Big Ones That Didn't Get Away!!

21" German Brown

19" German Brown

The Biggest Fish Yet...
22 in 4 lb Cutthroat
Strawberry Reservoir
Dec. 1998

First Day of Cub Scouts

Nov. 98

Ideas from Shirley

Shirley Pilkington (pictured with her granddaughter, Rose) attended Weber State University in Ogden, Utah, with an emphasis in Literature and English. Her poetry has been published on several occasions.

After only six months of scrapbooking, Shirley was hooked and opened up her own store, Daisy Dots & Doodles. She teaches scrapbooking classes several times a week and also designs scrapbook kits and papers. Shirley's own pages are full of texture and dimension and have been published in several scrapbook magazines.

Shirley lives in a beautiful rural town where she and her husband are active in their church and community. She is the mother of three children and the grandmother of six, which gives her a multitude of photo opportunities for her scrapbook pages.

Ralph J. Osmond Family
Donna, Lydia, Ralph, Dennis
Betty and Shirley

• Choose background paper carefully. Make certain that it will complement your photographs.

• Stickers can be used in a variety of ways. Cut them apart for even more possibilities. Foil stickers add shine to your pages.

• Run word strips around borders and make blocks to write journaling.

• Handmade tissue and paper add texture and dimension to pages. There are many different kinds available that are archival.

• When you are taking snapshots, move in close. Practice with a roll of film to see how close your camera will allow you to get for a great close-up picture.

Lydia Tullis

Lydia T. Osmond

The background papers in this double-page spread were softened by laying vellum over printed paper (below). Laser-cut photo corners give an antique look.

Ralph J Osmond

Ralph J Osmond

99

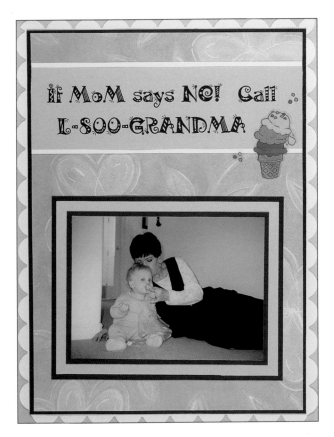

If MoM says NO! Call
1-800-GRANDMA

Using different fonts from your computer
makes titles more exciting and interesting
to look at (above).

Mack with his Gram and his cream puffs.

There's no place
Like home.....
Except Grandma's.

Sometimes a photograph taken from a different view, such as a back view (below),
captures a great memory.

GRANDMA SHIRLEY
This aint my first Rodeo...

Wishing You
Cowboy Spirit
AND
Christmas Cheer

Turkey, Pie,
SNOW

The background paper (above) was chosen specifically to complement the photograph.

Use circle and square cropped photographs on the same layout (below).

For candy corn, adhere three different sized and colored circles together. Cut the circle into eight pieces and mat each piece. Try to create other fun embellishments.

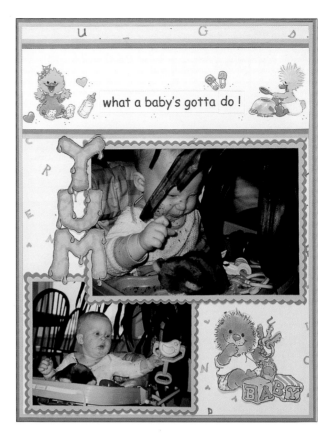

Brown glossy paper was used to cut out the chocolate bunny (below).

"A picture is worth a thousand words" holds true (above), so keep your camera ready.

So many toys, so little time!

Mack at Play...

Using a favorite nursery rhyme or song helps to capture a special memory (below).

The toy box (above) opens to display a photo or journaling.

Old MacDonald had a farm, Ee-igh, ee-igh, oh! And on that farm he had some chicks, Ee-igh, ee-igh, oh! With a chick-chick here, And a chick-chick there, Here

♪ Macky Storey had a farm Ee-igh, ee-igh, oh! ♪

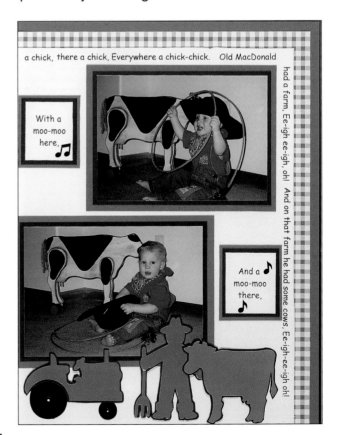

a chick, there a chick, Everywhere a chick-chick.   Old MacDonald had a farm, Ee-igh ee-igh, oh! And on that farm he had some cows, Ee-igh-ee-igh oh!

With a moo-moo here, ♪

And a moo-moo there, ♪

Matching mats on photographs and pages coordinates your layout (above).

Photographs of favorite places or things (below) will preserve cherished memories.

Letter stickers in different fonts and sizes make lettering easy and give your scrapbook pages a professional flair. Large letters lend themselves to this double-page spread.

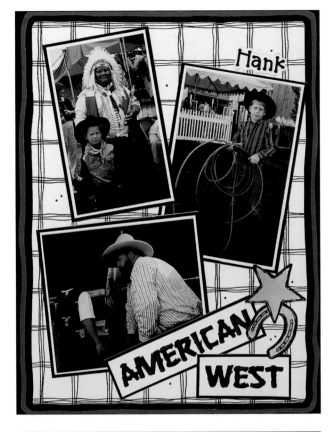

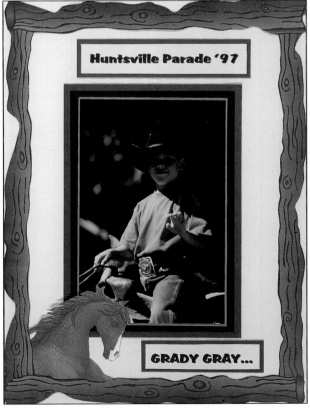

The fence in this double-page spread (below) is cut from textured brown paper to give it a "real" look. Twine was used for the rope. Be certain that any items used are archival.

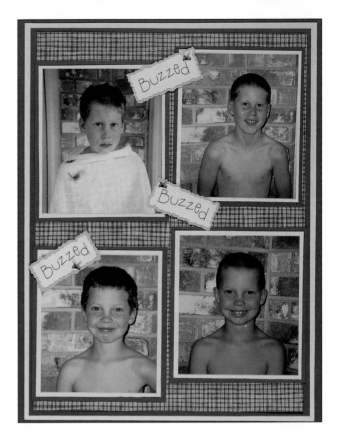

Punches and die-cuts were used to create the daisies (above).

Multiple mats (above) are pleasing to the eye and add interest to pages.

Acid-free adhesive spray was used to add a little splash of fine glitter. Die-cut lettering, confetti, and a basketball make these pages a celebration of fond memories.

Teddy Bear, Teddy Bear Buckaroo

(a "Beary", "Beary" special Boy & Bear)

A collection of stickers and paper cutouts make up this layout (above).

Try layering stickers. A cowboy hat was added to the bear sticker for fun (above).

Grady & Elli Summer 1998

WANTED

CAMPING

MITCH N' LONESOME

Mixing and matching coordinating prints are a fun way to highlight pages (below).

Bleeding embellishments off the page can create a different effect (below).

Make good use of a special card by cutting it out and using it to decorate scrapbook pages (below). Don't forget to use acid-free protection spray before you put it in your scrapbook.

Adhere stickers to colored paper. Leave a small border and trim. This will help to coordinate colors on a page or emphasize a favorite color.

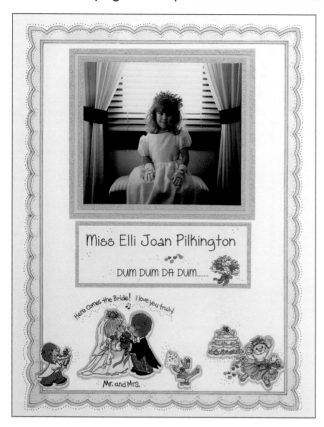

Mat your photographs and pages with a lacy look. Choose decorative-edged scissors that complement your photographs and cut all layers of double mats (below).

dum dum da dum

It's a Double Wedding!
Barbie and Rosebud

Her hair is all combed with pretty blonde curls,
She's all dressed in white as she dances and twirls,
My Barbie and I like to play and play,
Pretending like it is her wedding day.

This laser-cut frame (below) is oh-so-easy, but exceptionally effective.

The lace paper (below) was double mounted by trimming and staggering edges.

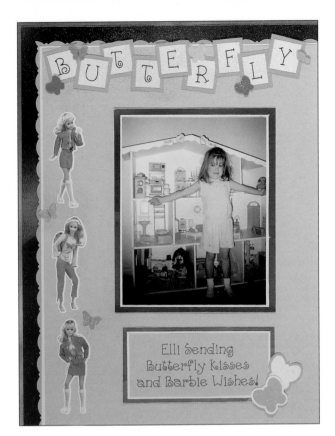

Try cutting your own block letters (above). Use a computer printout caption in your favorite font, stencils, or sticker letters. Cut into blocks and stagger them on your layout.

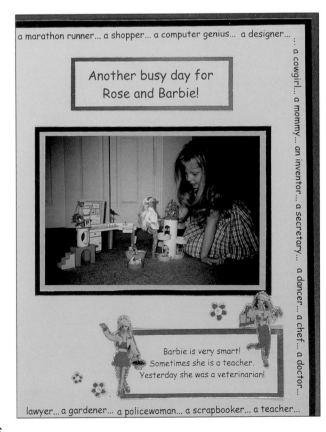

Self-adhesive foam will give dimension to accents (above).

Cutting stickers apart (below) gives you endless possibilities for accents.

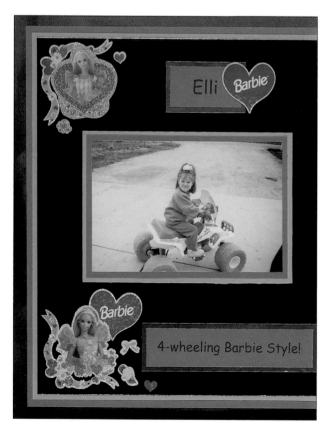

Decorative-edged scissors come in large and small patterns. Use a small pattern to create the mats for these pages (below).

Patterned and colored paper scraps are great for cutting out shapes (below).

Stickers make great accents, but they also make great backgrounds (above).

Take a small notebook on vacations to write down thoughts (below). This will assist when compiling scrapbooks.

Save memorabilia from vacations (below). With acid-free protection spray you can preserve additional interesting information.

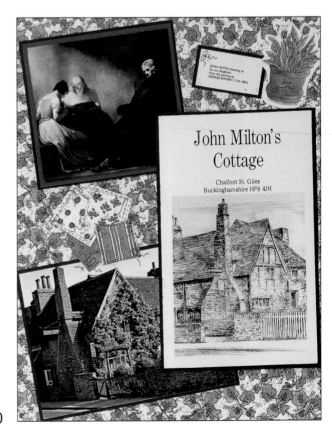

The floral arrangement (above) was made with punches from different colors of paper.

The close-up photo of the teacup (above) is one of a set purchased on this trip.

Holidays provide the perfect theme for a scrapbook page. Use bright colors, cut scraps of colored paper and create the perfect accent. Puffy stickers (above) are a unique way to give dimension to your holiday fun.

Here goes!

Go for it!

Give it all you've got!

Practice!
Practice!
Practice!

Wheeee!

HUMPH!

Oof!

You can do
Anything!

Diane &
Shirley...
"Cruis'n"

When the going gets tough,
the tough go on vacation!

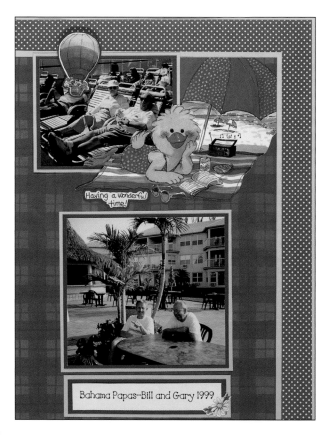

Having a wonderful
time!

Bahama Papas–Bill and Gary 1999

123

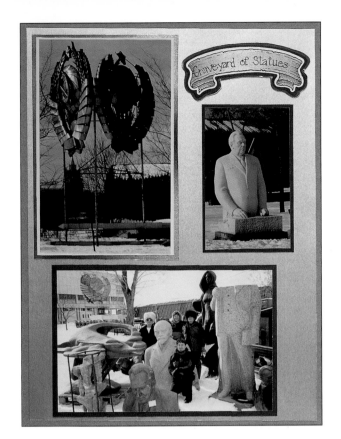

Notice the muted colors and simple design of these pages. The desire was to reflect the more serious, sober feelings that this trip evoked.

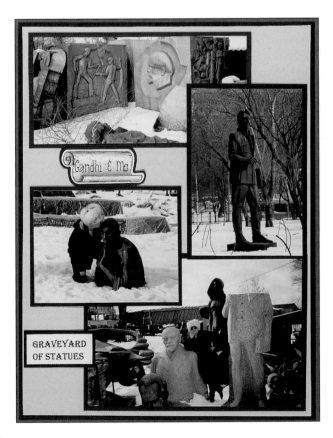

This double-page spread (below) uses computer clip art, die-cuts, sticky die-cuts, stencil lettering, and more. Notice the mats created with decorative-edged scissors to suggest alligator bites.

Tearing paper is an enjoyable technique that lets you create a unique shape. The background paper on this double-page spread (above) is a perfect complement for the winter photographs.

To highlight a special photograph, put it on a page all its own (above).

The textures of handmade paper leaves (below) are rich and give a look of fabric.

Index